# WITCHCRAFT
## What It Is and What It's Not

Witches have been victims of religious intolerance for centuries—even today, Witchcraft has an undeservedly negative reputation among the uninformed.

This book tells you why the propaganda about and misrepresentation of Witches as evil, Satan-worshipping cultists is absolutely false by enlightening you about the actual beliefs and practices of those who engage in the benign folk magic and religion of Witchcraft.

You will learn the difference between ceremonial magic, folk magic and religious magic; Wicca's stance as a non-organized, non-proselytizing religion; the real reasons for some Wiccans' use of ritual nudity and ritual sex; and the meaning of the Wiccans' one rule: "An it harm none, do what you will."

Witchcraft is rooted in a reverence for the Goddess and God through nature—but many falsehoods have been spread to discredit this life-affirming religion of individualists. *The Truth About Witchcraft* dispels the myths—so you can evaluate Witchcraft's beliefs for yourself.

## About the Author

Scott Cunningham practiced magic for over 20 years. He was the author of over 30 fiction and non-fiction books. Cunningham's books reflect a broad range of interests within the New Age sphere, where he was highly regarded. He passed from this life on March 28, 1993 after a long illness.

The Truth About

# WITCHCRAFT

by Scott Cunningham

2002
Llewellyn Publications
St. Paul, MN 55164-0383 U.S.A.

First Edition
Third Printing, 1992
Second Edition
Fourth Printing, 2002


International Standard Book Number:
0-87542-357-4


Llewellyn Publications
A Division of Llewellyn Worldwide, Ltd.
P.O. Box 64383, St. Paul, MN 55164-0383
www.llewellyn.com

Printed in the United States of America

# INTRODUCTION

Candles gleam. Incense smoke swirls. Robed figures, chanting in a long-dead language, whirl around a rustic wooden table. On it sit sacred images—a robust female wearing a crescent Moon on her forehead, a horned male holding a spear in his upraised hand.

All movement stops. A woman standing near the altar says:

> *In this sacred space and time*
> *we call now the Old Ones:*
> *The Goddess of the Moon, of seas and rivers;*
> *The God of the rayed Sun, of valleys and forests:*
> *Draw near us during this Circle.*

This is Witchcraft.

Two thousand miles away, a 15-year-old girl affixes a green candle onto a Polaroid photo of a friend. In the darkened room she lights the candle. Her eyes closed, the girl visualizes her boyfriend's broken arm surrounded by a purple light intended to quickly heal it.

This, too, is Witchcraft.

These two examples sum up Witchcraft. It is a religion, known as Wicca. It is also the practice of folk magic.

The average person probably thinks that Witchcraft is "Satanism," orgies and drug-ingesting. They falsely believe Witches to practice a mish-mash of "devil worship," unsavory rituals, cruelty and human sacrifice.

There certainly are people who do such things—murderers, psychotics and those frustrated by the religion into which they were born. But these people *aren't* Witches and they *don't* practice Witchcraft.

*The Truth About Witchcraft* examines both folk magic and the modern Wiccan religion, subjects long shrouded in secrecy. The lies have been told. It's time for the truth.

## BY CHARM AND SPELL

Folk magic was born in an age of wonder. Tens of thousands of years ago, nature was a mysterious force. Points of light swung far overhead in the sky. Invisible forces ruffled matted hair and kicked up dust storms. Water fell from above. Powerful forces, inconceivable to humans, sent flashes of light from the skies, blasting trees into raging infernos. Women miraculously bore young. All that moved eventually died. Blood was sacred. Food was sacred. Water, the Earth, plants, animals, the wind and all that existed was infused with power.

Magic—as well as religion and science—sprang from the actions of the first humans who tried to understand, contact and gain some control over such forces. Ritual developed as a means of uniting with the source of this universal energy. Gestures, rhythm, symbols, music, dance and the spoken word were used in ritual to shift the awareness to these higher powers.

Folk magic slowly developed from these beginnings. Every group, every tribe and civilization had its own forms of ritual. Folk magic differed from structured religion and state magic—this was the realm of personal magic, performed for personal reasons. A woman dressed a wound with a plantain leaf that she had gathered with her left hand to increase its healing properties. The fisherman rubbed his bone hooks with flowers to attract fish. Love-sick youths gathered heart-shaped stones and presented these to the objects of their desire.

These simple rituals continued to be used for many thousands of years, particularly in isolated areas. Then, a new organized religion, sprung up in the Near East after the death of a Jewish prophet, flexed its growing political muscles, sweeping across Europe. As country after country "converted," many of the old ways of folk magic were forgotten. Others were altered to outwardly conform to the new religion. That magic that could not be made to at least vaguely conform to the new religion was practiced in secret. The days were over when the old European charms and spells were a part of everyday life.

## SPELLS ON THE GALLOWS

Soon the leaders of the new religion, determined to wield absolute control over all aspects of human life, sought to stamp out such crimes of heresy as foretelling the future, psychic healing, spiritualism, the creation of protective amulets and love-attracting charms, and everything else which failed to fit in with this religion's creed.

Throughout the Western world, folk magic became a dim memory as scenes of religious mass-murders (performed in the name of "God") became commonplace.

Soon after, the era of scientific inquiry began. As the horrors of the Medieval and Renaissance "Witch" persecutions faded from the mind, humans began investigating the ways of nature. Magnetism, medicine, surgery, mathematics and astronomy were codified and moved from the realm of superstition and magic to science.

Building upon this knowledge, the Industrial Revolution began in the late 19th century. Humans had gained some control over the Earth and its energies, and machines soon replaced religion in overcoming folk magic.

In the 1900s, a series of local and world wars ripped apart much of what remained of the old ways of living for millions of Europeans and Americans. Folk magic, once the lifeblood of humans, had never seen darker days.

But it had not died out completely. Wherever machines and technology hadn't yet invaded, folk magic continued to exist. Throughout the Far, Near and Middle East, in Africa, Polynesia and Australia, in Central and South America, in rural sections of North America such as the Ozarks, in Hawaii and even in parts of Europe, folk magic still lived.

During the 1960s, folk magic sprang back into life. The youth movement in the United States and Britain rebelled against rigid social codes and

Christian-based ideals. Some young persons turned to Buddhism, Zen and other Eastern teachings. Others became entranced with what little they could learn of spells, charms, herb magic, tarot cards, amulets and talismans. Countless popular books and articles appeared, revealing this once-public knowledge to a new generation dissatisfied with its purely technological life.

Spellbooks and magical texts, written by researchers or practitioners of the old ways, were purchased by peoples whose ancestors had originated or preserved these vestiges of folk magic. Books such as Raymond Buckland's *Practical Candleburning Rituals* and dozens of other works were hugely successful. A reawakening of folk magic had begun.

## THE DEVIL'S WORK

The religious suppression of folk magic continued unabated during the 1960s. Books were released stating that this renewed interest in folk magic (often referred to as Witchcraft) heralded the end of the world. Preachers in the United States publicly burned occult books and magical objects. They did this, they said, in an attempt to destroy "the Devil's works."

However, Christianity's influence in shaping public opinion was weakening. Though many non-practitioners continued to view magic as "Satanic," unnatural and dangerous, open-minded persons investigated it for themselves. Some became ardent practitioners.

Today, the resurgence begun in the late 1960s has produced a generation of aware individuals. Many of these folk magicians also have become involved in channeling, psychic healing, herbal medicine, sensory deprivation, crystal consciousness, vegetarian diets, meditation and Asian teachings. This has produced the New Age movement.

As a response to the continuing interest in folk magic and non-Christian spirituality and to the waning of its social power, orthodox religion has now turned its propaganda guns toward this wave, again predicting that these are the last days of our planet.

## TODAY

Folk magic constitutes the bulk of ancient and modern magical techniques practiced by individuals to improve their lives.

What it *isn't* is almost as important as what it is. It isn't the "Devil's work." It isn't "Satanism." It doesn't involve sacrifices of humans or animals. It isn't talking to spirits or bondage to "demons." It isn't dark, dangerous or evil. Folk magic isn't anti-Christian, anti-religion or anti-anything.

Folk magic is pro-life, pro-healing, pro-love. It is a tool with which people can transform their lives. When normal means fail, when all efforts have brought no results, many millions today turn to folk magic.

It is practiced by 12-year-old girls and senior men and women. Professionals, laborers, lawyers and salespersons, all kinds of different people, perform spells.

Persons of every race carry out ancient rituals. Some of this is cultural. A Chicana living in southwestern Arizona might brush her children with rue and rosemary leaves to aid in healing them. A Creole man may stop by a shop to purchase a green candle and pine incense in preparation for a wealth-attracting ritual. Hawaiians plant hedges of *ki* (ti) plants around their homes for magical protection.

For others with no strong attachments to their ancestors, a plethora of spells and rituals are available for use in personal magic.

## THE SPELL

At the heart of folk magic is the spell. This is simply a ritual in which various tools are purposefully used, the goal is fully stated, and energy is moved to bring about the needed result.

Spells are usually misunderstood by non-practitioners. In popular thought, all you need to perform magic is a spell—a *real* spell, not the ones you find in books: a spell passed from an angel to King Solomon, a spell inscribed in some mythological 16th-century Welsh Witch's workbook, a spell of untold power. A few magical words, a dash of lizard's tongue and BAM! The magic is there. Your wildest dreams will be fulfilled—if only you have a real spell. Again, this is an outsider's idea.

In folk magic, spells—words, chants, gestures with tools—are the outer form only. The real magic, the movement of energy, is within the magician. No demonic power flows to help the spell-caster. Instead, the magician—by correctly performing a genuine spell—builds up the power within. At the proper time, this power is released to go to work in manifesting the spell.

Effective spells are designed to facilitate this. So, while "true" spells do exist, as well as many faultily composed ones, the actual magic isn't in the words or tools—it is within the folk magician. And as for ancient magic, "real" spells are being written every day. Old spells have no more power than new ones.

## TOOLS OF THE TRADE

Although personal power—that which resides within the magician—is the most potent force at work in folk magic, practitioners borrow freely from the spells and rituals of various cultures, utilizing a wide variety of magical equipment. These tools are used to lend their own energies to the ritual, as well as to put the magician in the proper frame of mind to perform the spell.

The tools of folk magic may be physical objects that can grasped in the hand. They also may be subtler, non-physical forces. These tools (along with suggestions for further reading regarding them) include:

*Quartz crystal and other minerals, gems and metals.* Currently, there is great interest in the United States concerning the metaphysical and magical uses of stones. Quartz crystals are worn by many to heighten their consciousness, while lapis lazuli is carried to increase psychic awareness. Michael G. Smith's *Crystal Power*, Diane Stein's *The Women's Book of Healing* and *Cunningham's Encyclopedia of Crystal, Gem and Metal Magic* are excellent guides to the uses of these tools.

*Colors.* The magical effects of color are startling. Folk magicians may change the color of their clothing to affect their moods. For example, blue clothing tempers heated emotions. An excellent guide to color magic can be found in Raymond Buckland's *Practical Color Magick.*

*Herbs, roots, oils and essences.* Rose petals are strewn around the home to promote peace or are placed near pink candles to bring love into the folk magician's life. Scott Cunningham's *Magical Herbalism* and *Cunningham's Encyclopedia of Magical Herbs* cover this subject. Ray T. Malbrough's *Charms, Spells and Formulas* and Cunningham's *The Magic of Incense, Oils and Brews* explore the magic of plant oils and incenses.

*Colored and shaped candles.* As outlined in Raymond Buckland's previously mentioned book, *Practical Candleburning Rituals,* inexpensive candles can be powerful focal points for personal power during folk magic rituals. Specific colors and shapes are utilized for their symbolic meanings and actual powers.

*Runes, images, symbols, pictures and gestures.* The magic of form is ancient, and these tools have long been used. *Earth Power* by Scott Cunningham contains traditional information regarding runes and image magic, as does *Buckland's Complete Book of Witchcraft.*

*Creative visualization.* The mind is a powerful force that the folk magician uses during spells. *The Llewellyn Practical Guide to Creative Visualization* by

Melita Denning and Osborne Phillips outlines specific visualization techniques. Indeed, most magical tools are unnecessary for magicians with properly trained minds.

*Elemental powers.* The use of the four elements in folk magic dates back to ancient Greece. Earth, Air, Fire and Water are powerful energy sources that folk magicians may tap into during rituals. *Earth Power* outlines many techniques to do just that.

*Food and cooking techniques.* Food has long been regarded as sacred and powerful. Some folk magicians today choose the foods they eat with magical goals in mind—such as eating chocolate to increase personal wealth. Ingesting specific foods to bring about magical changes is an old form of folk magic. Scott Cunningham's book, *The Magic of Food*, available from Llewellyn, will delve into this subject.

*Chants and poetry.* Words and chants help focus the magician's attention on the goal of the spell. The word "spell" originally referred to a ritual performed with spoken words. Poetry touches the subconscious mind and builds powers within the folk magician. Valerie Worth's now-classic *The Crone's Book of Words*, a collection of poem spells, reveals the magic of poetry. Chants are also included in *Practical Candleburning Rituals* and most folk magic works.

Many spells and rituals utilize two or more of these basic tools. For example, a simple peace-inducing spell might involve *blue candles*, *amethyst*, a handful of *rose petals* and a peaceful *chant*.

Since it is so intimately connected with nature, folk magic may take into account the following phenomena:

*Ocean tides, the weather, the seasons.* The high tide is the most auspicious time to perform folk magic for those living near the ocean. Electrical storms send extra energy to spells, and the seasons mark the ebb and flow of Earth Power. *Earth Power* by Scott Cunningham contains rituals involving the weather and the tides.

*Lunar phases.* Many magicians perform positive, beneficial spells or those designed to increase love, wealth and happiness during the waxing Moon, from the New Moon to the Full. Rituals involving the destruction of old, negative habits and weight loss spells may be cast during the waning Moon, from the Full to the New. Much traditional information regarding the Moon can be found in Llewellyn's *Moon Sign Book.*

*The time of day.* Some rituals are better performed after dark, while others are deemed most effective if timed with the rising of the Sun. Herbs, for example, are often picked at dawn so as to possess the magical forces of both the Moon (ruler of the night) and the Sun, the ruler of the day.

## THE GOALS OF FOLK MAGIC

Folk magic is often used in helping everyday problems of life. These include:

Prosperity, money and employment.
Peace, joy, happiness, friendships.
Love, fidelity and relationship troubles.
Sexuality problems.

Health and healing.
Protection.
Purification and exorcism.
Mental processes.
Overcoming negative habits.

In the past, folk magic was used to increase fertility, promote childbirth and influence powerful persons.

As I use this term, folk magic also includes divination, fortune telling and all other systems of discovering possible future trends or awakening our natural psychic awareness. They may utilize such tools as tarot cards, tea leaves and coffee grounds, the I Ching, flickering flames, rune stones, water, quartz crystal, beryl, shimmering or clear objects and dots and numbers. Forms of divination also involve observing chance occurrences, the movement of animals and birds, and clouds and weather phenomena.

From the range of tools and ritual purposes listed above, folk magic is obviously an extremely complex practice. Its very nature makes it personal. Due to such wide local and regional variations, most folk magic is difficult to discuss in general. Despite this, though, there are some basic principles that guide the folk magician.

## THE RATIONALE OF FOLK MAGIC

• There is a power in the universe.

This power is the inexplicable force behind the wonders that early humans encountered. The Earth, the solar system, the stars—all that is manifest—is a product of this power.

This power is also within all things. It is within humans, plants, stones, colors, shapes and sounds.

• This power can be roused and concentrated. Power is "awakened" and moved through ritual dance or other physical movement; through sounds such as music or chanting; through manipulation of various objects; through concentration or magical visualization.

• This power can be "programmed" with specific vibrations or energies to effect a specific result.

This result is the spell's purpose. It may be to speed healing, attract money or bring love into one's life. The power is programmed through the magician's visualization or the tools and ritual pattern chosen.

• This power can be moved and directed.

That power that exists within humans can be moved to other humans and to places and objects, and also transferred from objects to human beings.

It is moved and directed through visualization and with the use of tools such as images, wands, swords, pointed fingers and concentration.

• This power, once moved, has an effect on its target.

Once this power arrives at its destination, it changes the object, person or place. It accomplishes this due to its specific energies. The method by which the power changes its target is determined during ritual or is left up to circumstances at the time of its arrival.

This, in short, is the rationale of folk magic. Many of its practitioners aren't consciously aware of these ideas. Others certainly have different explanations and ideas concerning folk magic. However, broadly speaking, the only effective spells and rituals are those that are so constructed that any sufficiently involved magician, properly performing it, will raise energy, give it purpose ("program" it), direct it toward its goal and affect its target.

## MORALITY

If magicians perform effective magic, it follows that they must ensure that this power is properly used. Hence a type of "magical morality" exists. The fact that magicians are guided by any type of morality may seem surprising, but it is based on sound principles. The power at work in folk magic is just that—power. It is neither positive or negative, "good" nor "evil." Only the intention and goal of the magician working with it determines whether this energy is used for helpful or harmful ends.

Contrary to popular belief, folk magicians do not cast spells to manipulate, hurt, injure, or kill others. Practitioners of folk magic usually perform the craft for positive reasons. Certainly, it is untrue to say that *all* practitioners use folk magic in non-harmful ways, just as the statement "all chefs use their knives solely for chopping onions"' is untrue. However, those few practitioners of negative (harmful) magic are violating the basic principle of folk magic: *Harm none.*

This premise, the idea behind most religious and civil codes of conduct, is universal. Harm none means just that—no one. Not yourself, not your enemies, no one. Harming includes physical, emotional, mental, spiritual and psychic damage. Manipulation of others is included in this, as is harming the Earth and its treasures.

After suffering through centuries of a well-crafted disinformation campaign waged by organized religion, many still believe that all magic is harmful. This is only natural, but it is false. The so-called evil magicians do exist, but they are rare. Why? Either they find easier means to do their dirty work or they simply aren't around for long.

Magic is not a short cut. The projection of energy is an expenditure of the life force within. Beating up your enemy or sleeping with his or her mate is far easier than performing destructive magic. The reasons why this "harm none" rule exists are, in brief:

*Magicians respect life.* All living creatures—including humans and animals—are manifestations of the universal power. As such, they are respected—not hurt.

*Magicians respect the Earth.* Long revered in religions throughout history around the world, the Earth is respected as the most intense manifestation of energy within our reach. It is also a source of incredible power. As such, magicians "walk gently" upon our home.

*Magicians respect the power.* As the ultimate, universal force, the power is inconceivable. The energy that created galaxies, DNA, humans and billions of forms of terrestrial plants isn't something to challenge. It is even more unwise to misuse the power. Most folk magicians aren't *afraid* of the power; they wisely respect it.

Reverence of this energy is the basis of all religion. It is that which has been called God, Jehovah, Yemaya, Goddess, Isis and every other human conception of the divine.

To misuse this power (i.e., to rouse and direct it for destructive ends) is to set up a negative current of energy. Once this has begun, once a magician has wreaked metaphysical havoc, there is no turning back. The current is closed. In programming personal energy with negativity, the magician infuses individual power by unlocking it within. It soon overcomes the magician.

## WHEN ALL ELSE FAILS

The second major rule of folk magic is: Use magic when all else fails.

And so, energy isn't directed to open a door, wash the dishes or start a car without a key. At the physical level, folk magic is usually used only as a last resort or in emergencies when other means aren't available. Why? Personal power is limited. We can't constantly release large amounts of our energy without suffering negative side effects. If the magician is unaware of the methods to recharge personal power by receiving energy from the Earth, this deficiency may manifest as general weakness, anemia and disease.

So, while not a misuse, working folk magic for easily solved problems (or, worse, to impress peers) is a waste of time and energy. Folk magic exists to help humans with the countless problems of life that cannot be answered by "normal" physical means, but folk magic is not a panacea.

## DOES IT WORK?

Folk magic has been practiced, as we've seen, for tens of thousands of years. It is still used today by intelligent persons as well as by the ignorant. Some say its continuance is due to its practitioners' desperate need to *believe* that it is effective. Others (folk magicians) say that it's still with us because it works.

Such a point can be argued endlessly. Those who have used folk magic to manifest needed results don't need further convincing. Those who haven't practiced it—or who have done so unsuccessfully— are unwilling to admit that it could possibly be effective.

Folk magic is there for those who desire to practice it. Folk magic serves the need for individual humans to take control of their lives. This isn't through the manipulation of nature, through domination or commandeering. Instead, magicians work *with* nature's powers and their own personal energy.

That aspect of Witchcraft termed folk magic is a power of the people, not of organized religion, nor politics, authority or groups. This has sustained it through the millennia. Among some of its practitioners, it is a continuance of tradition and culture, a link with ancestors long gone, an affirmation of cultural worth. This, too, is a reason for its survival.

Yes, folk magic works. Ask its practitioners. But it has no monopoly on wisdom—the techniques used in folk magic are no more or less effective than those used in ceremonial magic or religion-based magic. The aims and tools of folk magic may be different, but the results are the same.

## FOLK VS. CEREMONIAL

Ceremonial (ritual) magic is a contemporary system built around ancient Sumerian, Egyptian, Indian and Semitic magic, with influences of Arabic and later Christian thought. Masonry also contributed to the present structure of ceremonial magic, as did the secret societies that were popular in Great Britain and throughout Europe in the late 1700s.

The tools, ritual structures, terminology and goals of ceremonial magic are usually—but not always—centered around the goal of union with the divine, with perfection and expanded consciousness. Or, as it is commonly described, knowledge of and conversation with your holy guardian angel.

Speaking generally (always a dangerous act), ceremonial magic isn't concerned with the aims of folk magic: love, healing, money, happiness and joy. When these needs are addressed through ceremonial magic, it is as a means to an end—the attainment of the union mentioned above. In contrast, folk magicians solve problems with their rituals and rarely look further.

Unlike folk magic, ceremonial magic is usually religious in nature. While its practitioners may not subscribe to any current religious philosophy, they are certainly concerned with contacting and becoming one with Deity, however it is visualized. Because of this, they borrow deity forms and ritual patterns from past and present religions.

Some ceremonial groups, such as *The Golden Dawn*, drew upon Egyptian mythology when devising their magical workings. Many of the rituals used by a splinter group of this magical lodge of the late 1800s and early 1900s have been published in *The Golden Dawn* by Israel Regardie, perhaps one of the most influential magical books ever printed.

The classical grimoires, or magical workbooks, of the Middle Ages and the Renaissance include invocations to Jehovah, Adonai, God and other Judaic/Christian beings. This isn't heresy or mockery, but the product of a different interpretation of the Christian mythos. This is far from folk magic, in which the power is sent without invocation to divinities. In this area, folk magic and ceremonial magic have little in common.

For more information regarding contemporary ceremonial magic, consult *Modern Magick* by Don Kraig; Donald Tyson's *The New Magus*, Denning & Phillips' *Mysteria Magica* and Regardie's *The Golden Dawn*.

## RELIGIOUS MAGIC

Religious magic is that which is performed in the name of, or with the assistance of, deities. It has been practiced by peoples all over the world, at all times in history.

In earlier ages, deities of the fields, the mountains, springs and woods were invoked during magic. The Moon and Sun were thought of as deities (or representations of them), and were called upon during magical ritual. This was, perhaps, the purest form of religious magic.

Prayer is, essentially, a rite of magic. When an individual fervently prays, asking for a blessing, or a new car, or a caring husband or wife, the devout person (unknowingly) directs personal power through the prayer and out to the deity. The person's emotional involvement in the prayer "programs" it. This is done on the assumption that the deity will send the energy to the correct place and so bring the prayer into manifestation.

Sometimes this divine power is brought down through the agency of a priest or minister, and is made to enter certain objects. This form of religious magic includes the creation and use of blessed religious medallions, crucifixes and palm leaves worn by some Catholics for special favors. It is also the rationale of transubstantiation.

An extreme example of unorthodox religious magic (i.e., that not performed by priests or other church officials) is the common medieval practice of stealing blessed hosts from Catholic churches for use in love spells, healing rituals and so on. *This was done by persons who had forgotten folk magic—not by Witches. Witches had their own magic.* It certainly wasn't a mockery of Catholicism or Christianity. On the contrary, it was an acknowledgement of the power of the religion and its priests.

Once Christianity had established itself throughout Europe, some folk magicians nudged their way toward religious magic. Whether this was an attempt to save their necks or was the result of their true conversion to the new faith is still open to speculation.

At one time, a woman wishing to prepare an herbal charm to protect her child would collect herbs while chanting ancient words, calling on the plant to make its sacrifice for the benefit of humans. She'd fasten the herbs in cloth and hang this charm around her child's neck.

After Christianity's rise to power, the herbs were plucked with prayers to Jesus, God or the Virgin Mary. Saints were often invoked (at least by Catholics). The cloth may have been stitched with a cross, symbol of the new religion. Finally, the "magic charm" was taken to a church to be blessed by a priest. This marked the movement of much folk magic into the realms of religious magic.

Lighting a candle to a deity and asking for a favor is another form of religious magic, as is any other type performed with supplications or invocations to higher powers, such as modern Wiccan magic.

Religious magic, naturally, is frowned upon by officials of the religions in question. Rome can't be too happy that many Mexican-Americans wear medals depicting the saints for magical purposes, but they do. An introduction to Mexican-American magic can be found in M. V. Devine's *Brujeria: A Study in Mexican-American Folk Magic*. The complexity of magic is apparent in this unusual book title.

Any form of folk magic can be performed by ceremonial magicians or in a religious context. When this occurs, it ceases to be folk magic.

## THE CONTINUATION

Folk magic isn't religious and it isn't ceremonial magic. It stands on its own as a practice worked by persons unafraid to delve farther than others into the mysteries of nature, than others, who are unwilling to let life overwhelm them when problems arise.

As one of the major components of Witchcraft, folk magic is deeply rooted in our consciousness. Even those who profess no occult beliefs or interest in magic may practice it. The notion that wearing lucky ties will ensure successful business transactions is still alive. So too is the idea that wearing a certain dress (blouse, sweater, shoes) on a date will ensure a woman's chances of finding the right mate. Good luck charms are still carried by serious-minded individuals. Positive thinking is simply a form of mental folk magic. Many millions look to divination to answer questions regarding the future.

Vestiges of ancient folk magic linger in our everyday lives. Blowing out candles on a birthday cake, wishing on stars, tossing coins into wells, clinking glasses during toasts and countless other minor rituals are still practiced much as they were when they were created.

Folk magic didn't die out with persecutions or with religious campaigns, nor did wars or the Industrial Revolution stamp it out. It is alive today, helping people who help themselves.

## WICCA

Folk magic—the magic of the people—is but half of what is termed Witchcraft. The other half is the religion known as Wicca. Wicca is not religious magic, though its practitioners are involved in magic. It isn't a magical religion either. Wicca is a religion that embraces magic, welcomes it and practices it—but magic isn't at the heart of Wicca.

Current Western religion, say the Wiccans, is out of balance. Deity is usually referred to as God, as opposed to Goddess. God the Father is a common term. The concept of male saviors, directly descended from male divinities, is widespread, even outside Christianity. Religious officials, such as priests and ministers, are usually male, though this is slowly changing as women demand a voice in spirituality. Contemporary religions focus much of their attention on *maleness*.

The Wiccans are different. They view nature as a manifestation of deity. Because of this, they believe that a male divinity revered without a female deity is, at best, only half correct. Both sexes exist in nature. If nature is a manifestation of divinity, then divinity also manifests itself in male and female forms. Hence, modern Wicca usually is centered around reverence of the Goddess and the God as aspects of the universal power. *Both*; not one, not the other.

Such a concept is certainly not new. Ancient religions are replete with deities of both sexes. Faiths in many parts of the world today are also in line with this concept. Where ancient religions still thrive, unhindered by the effects of well-meaning but culture-destroying "missionaries," goddesses and gods are still worshiped.

And so Wicca is a religion built around these twin deities, the Goddess and the God. These divinities are thought to be twin energies or nonphysical manifestations of the power that was discussed in the Folk Magic section in this booklet.

Just as early peoples began practicing folk magic, so too did some begin to sense presences or personalities within this force. This was the advent of all religion. Wicca is in harmony with ancient religious practices and beliefs. It isn't a step backward, nor is it a slap in the face of Christianity or any other contemporary, male-based religion. Wicca is an alternative religion, one that is fulfilling to its adherents.

## WITCH!

Now, to turn to the feared, ridiculed, wrongly used word *Witch*. Witches, people will still tell you, are ugly old women who have sold their souls to the Devil, who work to destroy Christianity, kill their babies and eat lizards for lunch. Additionally, it is thought that Witches belong to an organized Satan-worshipping church.

Many holding this idea seem to actually believe such persons exist. Where did this concept come from? Right—from the same religious campaign that vowed to end the practice of folk magic. When a religion wages war, it does so ruthlessly. Think about the current situations in the Middle East and Northern Ireland. Though much more than religion is involved in these examples, it is at the heart of the conflicts. Both sides in a religious war believe that God is on their side.

Many individuals believe that such bizarre persons—the stereotypical Witch—actually existed and still do. There may have been some women who fit the bizarre image of a Witch—crazed individuals who, with nothing else to strike out at, turned against conventional religion and their own families. Through a mixture of fantasy and psychosis, they became the characters that Christianity had invented. But they were not Witches.

An organized, structured, anti-Christian religion involved with "Devil worship"—as described by Christians past and present—has never existed and still doesn't. After all, only a Christian can believe in the Devil.

Wiccans have their own beliefs and rituals that are totally unrelated to Christianity. So, Wiccans don't sell their souls to the devil, nor are they trying to corrupt the world.

The charges of Witches (Wiccans) killing their babies are absurd, since Wiccans, in common with folk magicians, *respect the life force*. They don't kill babies, or anything else. So this concept of Witch is false.

Some Wiccans don't use the word Witch to describe themselves. After centuries of negative associations with this term, they prefer Wiccan. Other Wiccans proudly call themselves Witch, even in television interviews and on book covers. More confusing still, many practitioners of folk magic are self-professed Witches who have no Wiccan affiliations.

Witchcraft, properly, is the craft of the Witch. This craft is folk magic. Some Wiccans extend this to include the religious rituals of Wicca; hence, Witchcraft is magic and ritual. Wiccans may call themselves Witches, but folk magicians rarely describe themselves as Wiccan. Hence, Wiccans are those who practice the religion of Wicca, whether or not they also term themselves Witch.

## THE RELIGION OF WICCA

Religions are organizations dedicated to revering deities. Most Wiccans revere the Goddess and the God but there are tremendous differences in the basic beliefs and ritual practices of contemporary Wiccans.

The Goddess and the God are the primal female and male forces. They are, in a sense, two equal but opposite aspects of the universal power. Wiccan ritual celebrates them. There are myths in which the Goddess and God play their roles. These are usually related to the seasons, to the Sun and Moon. Some Wiccan myths resemble ancient Sumerian and Greek stories of deities.

Contained within the Goddess and God are all the deities that ever were. The Goddess is the female force, the Maiden, Mother and Crone. She is all-woman, all-fertility. She is seen in the Moon, the waters, in love and life. The God is the male force. He is the horned hunter and the grain in the fields. He is seen in the Sun and in fire, passion and life.

Wiccans often develop personal relationships with the Goddess and God. These aren't cold, distant deities that exist somewhere in space. They are as real as rain, wind and the Earth. These are the deities revered within Wicca—not Satan, the Devil or any other Christian concepts or beings.

## INITIATION

In the past, Wicca was primarily a secret, initiatory religion. In this traditional Wicca, most practitioners were members of covens—groups of Wiccans who met for study, worship and magic. Some of these covens were primarily training organizations with varying memberships. Others retained cohesive group identities and rarely allowed new members to join. This is still true today, but many non-traditional covens now exist. Some are non-initiatory, others self-initiatory.

Covens are usually limited to 13 members but may have fewer. This number is symbolic of the Lunar months. It is also, as is frequently said, the maximum number of persons capable of easily fitting into the ritual space, the "magic circle" or sphere created prior to every Wiccan rite. Unlike many other traditions, Wiccans don't build physical buildings in which to worship. Most traditional covens are led by a high priestess and high priest. These are generally Wiccans who, after years of Wiccan training and experience, have undergone three separate initiations, permitting them to lead a coven and to teach Wicca to others.

Traditional initiation rituals are usually dramatic experiences. If the ceremony is properly enacted, the person undergoing the ritual is profoundly changed—

emerging with a new identity as a member of the Craft, as Wicca is often termed. Such initiation ceremonies are universal, in secret and magical groups. In Wicca, the initiation ritual is designed not only to present the person to the Goddess and God as a Wiccan, but also to expand her or his awareness of other states of consciousness and the reality of non-physical energies. The candidate may undergo some type of symbolic death (such as being covered with a thick, black cloth) only to be "reborn" into Wicca. The initiate may be given a Wiccan name and presented with magical tools. Finally, the new Wiccan is presented to the Goddess and God.

Though many Wiccan initiations are secret, many others have been published and are available for study. The words alone in such rituals are merely echoes of the magic that is at work during true initiation.

## TRADITIONS

Wiccan traditions (or loosely organized groups of covens) are varied, though most subscribe to basic Wiccan philosophy. Some were founded or popularized by now near-legendary Wiccan figures in the recent past. Many are linked with a specific culture or country. British traditions often invoke Brythonic deities such as Kerridwen, Kernunnos, Dagda, Tara and many others. Greek or Roman-oriented traditions might call upon Diana, Pan, Faunus and Demeter. The names Wiccans give to the Goddess and God aren't important; they are simply keys to contacting and communing with the deities.

Each tradition possesses its own set of rituals, laws and magical rites, often peculiar to that tradition alone. This information is usually contained within a *Book of Shadows*. In the past this book—the key to the tradition— was hand copied by each new initiate after their admittance to the coven. This is still true today, but many non-traditional groups photocopy the book. Others (particularly solitary Wiccans) may compose their own.

A wide variety of ritual practices are found in different Wiccan traditions, and there's often little agreement on various aspects of ceremony. For example, some traditions focus on Goddess worship and relegate the God to the role of consort. Many traditions are robed, while others practice ritual nudity. Despite these differences, there's little infighting among Wiccans. In general, no one tradition believes it is the only Wiccan way.

The 1980s have seen the birth of new non-traditional forms of Wicca. Many are turning their backs on secrecy, initiatory rituals and organized, hierarchical covens. Wiccans are performing self-initiations rather than receiving them from others. Old ritual forms are being laid aside in favor of spontaneity. And many Wiccans now choose to practice their religion alone.

## THE LONE WICCA

There have always been lone Wiccans, or solitaries. These are usually persons who have been dissatisfied with covens or who have been unable to contact a secret group.

Until recently, solitary Wiccans who hadn't received initiation practiced their religion as best they could, taking hints from books and lectures. One of the earliest of these source books was Raymond Buckland's *Witchcraft from the Inside*. This is a coherent account of Gardnerian Wicca, one of the major British traditions. No Wiccan "training manuals" had yet been openly published, and most covens were still wary of handing their rituals over to non-initiates.

This is in the past. Many qualified Wiccan authors, agreeing with the ideals of the current movement of non-traditional Wicca, have produced books containing a wealth of traditional as well as contemporary Wiccan information. Many offer complete rituals and training instructions.

One of these is *Buckland's Complete Book of Witchcraft*. Written by Raymond Buckland, one of the early public Wiccan figures in the United States, it is a guide to the basic aspects of the Wiccan religion. The book also contains much of the folk magic commonly performed by Wiccans.

Acknowledging the need for reliable texts for solitary Wiccans, Scott Cunningham has completed a book entitled *Wicca: A Guide for the Solitary Practitioner*. This book, published by Llewellyn, contains a new Book of Shadows for the interested student to use in learning and experiencing Wicca, and in structuring a personal Wiccan tradition.

## WOMEN'S SPIRITUALITY

With the birth of the true women's liberation movement in the 1960s, many women became disenchanted with orthodox religion. Some found Wicca and began yet another non-traditional form—Feminist, or Women's Wicca.

Spearheading this movement was the publication of Z. Budapest's *The Feminist Book of Lights and Shadows*, later revised and published as *The Holy Book of Women's Mysteries Volume 1*. A second volume also was published.

1987 saw publication of Diane Stein's *The Women's Spirituality Book*. This work delves into Goddess spirituality and women's Wicca, and also contains much magical information.

Many women see Wicca as an ideal religion, for it acknowledges and reveres the feminine aspect of Deity. Some feminist covens have become heavily involved in politics in an effort to secure women's deserving equality in society. Many are active in anti-nuclear campaigns.

Some feminist covens are "women only" groups, and may not even invoke the God in their rituals. This is the result of thousands of years of male-oriented religion. While such groups are certainly Wiccan, they are as unbalanced, spiritually speaking, as those religions solely worshipping a male deity. Other all-women covens recognize the God—often as an aspect of the Goddess.

However, most Wiccans will affirm that the Goddess and the God are equal but separate halves of a whole: that undefinable, universal, omnipresent power source. In Wicca today, there's room for every school of thought.

Though feminist Wicca was once viewed as upstart and non-traditional (i.e., non-valid) by traditional Wiccans, it has settled into its own space and is now a growing and influential movement within Wicca. It is certainly fulfilling a need for women to rediscover the Goddess within.

## THE WICCAN YEAR

All religions have sacred calendars containing various days of power or times associated with particular deities. Most Wiccans perform rituals at least 21 times a year: 13 Full Moon celebrations, usually Goddess-oriented, and eight Sabbats, or solar festivals, related to the God. Some Wiccans meet with their covens for these rites, while others perform them alone.

The Moon is an ancient symbol of the Goddess. Countless religions have recognized the moon with rites and ceremonies. Contemporary Wiccans often gather (if coven members) on the nights of the Full Moon each month for worship and magical ritual.

The Sabbats are seasonally based. They are connected with old European planting and harvesting times as well as with hunting rites.

In essence, the Sabbats tell the story of the God and the Goddess. In festival form they reveal a seasonal and agricultural Wiccan legend. Four of them are related to the astronomical solstices and equinoxes.

Briefly, here are the eight Sabbats of Wicca and some of the generally accepted symbolism of each. The names for the various festivals differ greatly from tradition to tradition; the ones used here are those most commonly found in British-based Wiccan groups.

## SAMHAIN TO MABON

Many Wiccans begin their year with *Samhain* (October 31). On this night they revere their friends and loved ones who have passed on to the other life. Because Wiccans accept the doctrine of reincarnation, this isn't a completely somber festival. Many Wiccans also mark the symbolic death of the Horned God on this night. Samhain is linked with the coming of winter and ancient hunting rituals.

*Yule* (*circa* December 21; the actual date varies yearly) celebrates the rebirth of the God through the agency of the Goddess. It is life amid the seeming death of winter. This isn't a mockery of Christianity's holy day. The Winter Solstice is an ancient Pagan festival that early Christian leaders adopted as the symbolic date of Jesus birth.

*Imbolc* (February 1 or 2) is the time when the Goddess has, symbolically, recovered from giving birth to the God. It is a festival of purification and fertility.

*Ostara* (*circa* March 21), the Spring Solstice, marks the first day of true spring. It is a time of the awakening of the Earth (the Goddess) as the Sun (the God) grows in power and warmth.

April 30 is celebrated as *Beltane*. On this festival the young God ventures into manhood. He and the Goddess (His mother/lover) join and produce the bounty of nature. This isn't incest; it is nature symbolism. In Wiccan thought the Goddess and God are one, united. They are dual reflections of the power behind the universe.

*Midsummer* (*circa* June 21) is the point at which the powers of nature are at their peak. Wiccans gather to celebrate and to practice magic.

*Lughnasadh* (August 1) is the harvest's beginning. The God weakens as the first grains and fruits are cut. Lughnasadh is celebrated as a thanks ritual.

*Mabon* (*circa* September 21) is the second harvest. The God prepares to leave His life behind Him as the last fruits are gathered to nourish all peoples. The warmth is lessening day by day.

Samhain follows Mabon, and the cycle of rituals is completed.

## WICCAN RITUAL TOOLS

Religion is reverence of Deity. Various tools, symbols and rituals are utilized in this reverence. Some of these are used for magical purposes.

Wicca, as a religion centered around the Goddess and the God, uses unique tools, symbols and ritual structures. Most of these aren't found in any other contemporary religion. Most Wiccan tools are used by all traditions but the following information is a generalization, drawn from a number of Wiccan traditions. Many differences exist from group to group. There is no universality in Wiccan rituals.

At the center of Wiccan ceremonies is the altar. This may be a table, a rock, a tree stump, a cleared area of the ground. On the altar various tools are placed. These may include:

*Images of the Goddess and God.* These range from carved wooden figures to abstract representations such as round stones, acorns and other natural symbols. Some Wiccans utilize two candles to represent the deities. In any case, the images aren't viewed as the abodes of the Goddess and God; they are simply symbols.

The *athame*, or ritual knife. It is a black-handled knife that isn't used for sacrifice. In fact, most Wiccans never use the athame for cutting purposes. It is a tool utilized to direct power from the body to the outside world. The athame is symbolic of the God in some Wiccan traditions. A sword may be used in place of the athame.

The *wand* is much like those used by early ceremonial magicians. It is often fashioned of wood and may be engraved with symbols or studded with stones. Some are made of silver. The wand is an instrument of invocation, of inviting the deities' presence during ritual.

The *cauldron* is a large metal vessel, usually made of iron. It is seen to be symbolic of the Goddess. Fires may be lit within it, or the cauldron may be filled with water and flowers. Despite popular misconceptions, brews are rarely created in the cauldron.

The *pentacle* is a flat piece of metal, clay, wood or some other natural substance. On it are engraved or carved various symbols. One of these is the pentagram, the five-pointed star used in ancient magic. (Contrary to what television evangelists and radical Christians have been recently preaching, the pentagram is not a Satanic symbol.) The pentacle is sometimes used as a base on which other tools or objects are placed while being charged with energy during a ritual.

The *cup*, or chalice, is another Goddess symbol. It may contain wine or water that is ritually imbibed.

The *censer* is an incense burner. In common with ancient religions, Wiccans usually burn incense during ritual in honor of the deities.

*Bowls of salt and water* are frequently encountered on Wiccan altars. Mixed together, these two substances form a purifying liquid that may be sprinkled around the ritual area.

*Cords* of various natural materials may be present on the altar. Though the symbolism of cords varies, it usually signifies the material world and manifestation. They also symbolize of the bond of the members to the coven and that between the deities and the Wiccans.

The *broom* is sometimes used as a tool of purification, to ritually sweep the area prior to working. Afterward, it may be laid against the altar.

Other objects sometimes found on the altar include a quartz crystal sphere, symbolic of the Goddess and used in awakening psychic powers; *fresh flowers or greens*, representing the bounty of nature; *bells and other musical instruments*, which are used to create sacred music; *mirrors* or other reflecting surfaces that are Goddess-symbolic, and many other items.

The bulk of these tools are used in ritual for various purposes, among these being:

*To create the area of worship.* Since Wiccans rarely have buildings set aside solely for ritual workings, sacred space is created at each ritual. The athame and, sometimes, the wand are used for this purpose. The salt and water as well as the broom may be used to purify the area. The censer is also at work here, for it creates the appropriate atmosphere through scent.

*To invoke the presence of the Goddess and God during ritual.* The wand is the primary tool used here.

*To serve as focal points for power during magic.* This may be the quartz crystal sphere or an object lying on top of the pentacle. Some groups utilize the cauldron.

*To direct energy toward its destination.* The athame is the most widely used tool of energy direction.

Some Wiccans won't allow others to handle their tools. They are sacred in that they have been set aside for ritual purposes. They may be kept in storage and taken out only for specific use. Others constantly utilize their tools, believing that the more they work with them (even in non-ritual capacities), the more effective they will be in their hands and with their energy.

## WICCAN RITUALS

The rituals of Wicca are varied. Particular Wiccan traditions have specific ritual patterns that are often rigidly followed. Other, non-traditional Wiccans may create new rituals for each occasion. And some groups (or individuals) perform spontaneous rites, chanting or moving or speaking as they feel compelled.

A few basic ritual components are found within most Wiccan rituals. Again, there are many variations; these are generalizations only. Most workings begin with the creation of sacred space. This is often termed the magic circle, the circle of power or the sphere of power. Basically, this is the creation of a sphere of energy surrounding the ritual area. This sphere is created by moving personal power out from the body, directing it through the athame, and then, through visualization, forming it into a glowing energy sphere that encompasses the ritual area. Half of this sphere is above the ground, the other half below. The place where this large energy sphere cuts into the ground (or floor) marks the magic circle—-hence, this name.

This circle is deemed the most fit place to honor the Goddess and God. During magic it contains and concentrates energy until it is released toward its goal.

Once the sphere has been formed, the actual rituals begin.

## THE FOUR QUARTERS

Directly after forming the magic circle, many Wiccans perform invocations to the four quarters—that is, the four directions. Watchtowers or Kings or Queens of the Elements may be called to be in attendance during the ritual for protective purposes or to lend their special energies. In some groups, these four invocations may be said by four individuals, while in others the high priestess or high priest may do this.

Next, or sometimes prior to this, the Goddess and God are invoked to witness the rituals. *How* they are invoked is up to the group or individual involved. Most rely on words; others may chant, sing, make music or dance. The form isn't important. What *is* important is that the invocations are successful.

Some Wiccans see the Goddess and God as descending from above to be present at the rites. Others view them as residing in the Earth and call them from there. More commonly, the Goddess and God are thought to be residing within, and the invocation is merely a tool that the Wiccans use to become newly aware of their presence.

Once they have been invoked, the actual workings begin. If this meeting is a Sabbat, a seasonal ritual usually is performed. This may involve spoken passages, enactments of myths and dramatic demonstrations of the season's attributes, such as scattering autumn leaves or laying spring flowers around the magic circle or on the altar.

If the ritual is an Esbat, an invocation is spoken, sung or chanted to the Goddess in Her Lunar aspect, and then magical workings begin.

On Sabbats, the seasonal rites precede the magic, if they are done at all. Afterward, some Wiccans practice various forms of divination. Samhain is one Sabbat at which this is usually done.

Following this comes a simple ritual meal. This usually consists of wine, ale or fruit juice and crescent-shaped cakes. Far from enacting a mockery of the Christian communion, Wiccans are following the forms of ancient Middle Eastern and Greek rituals in which such meals—including the crescent cakes—were enjoyed. When a coven gathers for a Sabbat, a feast often occurs, created with the dishes that members have brought.

After the meal, the magic sphere is "broken" or "opened." This is the ceremonial dispersing of the power that created it. The ritual is done. That's about it. No pacts with the Devil, no orgies, no sacrifices, no dark dealings with demons.

## TO ROBE OR NOT?

One of the major areas in which Wiccans have been attacked is their use of ritual nudity. Many Wiccans practice nudity during ritual. This is the antithesis of wearing your Sunday best, a doing away with the elaborate ritual attire often worn in other religions.

But many other Wiccans—perhaps the majority—wear robes during rituals. Some even go into the circle in street clothing.

Outsiders point to Wiccan ritual nudity and sneer, saying "See? They're naked. That *proves* that they have orgies!"

Well—

Many doctors, lawyers, business persons and members of orthodox religions are nudists, but few accuse them of indulging in devil worship or orgies. The false belief that social nudity inevitably leads to sex is the result of 2,000 years of prudery, fostered by a new religion determined to erase all traces of Paganism.

Any rational, well-adjusted person who has visited a nude beach, a clothing-optional resort or nudist camp realizes that nudity soon loses its novelty. When persons are naked for reasons other than sex, the arousal quotient quickly vanishes.

Some Wiccans say that all their rituals in the past were conducted without clothing. This simply isn't true. Though ritual nudity has a long history in parts of Europe, India, Polynesia, among some American groups and even in planting rites of the Ozark Mountains, most of Europe was far too cold for such practices.

Some Wiccans perform rituals nude because they see it as being natural. Others don't take off their clothing because they prefer not to.

Wicca, as has been frequently mentioned, is a religion of individualism.

## SEX AND WITCHCRAFT

Any mention of the word Witchcraft usually brings to mind orgies. Sex and Witchcraft, outsiders believe, are inextricably linked.

This isn't true.

Some Wiccans do utilize sex in rituals. This may occur during third degree initiation ceremonies, which are rare and are granted only after years of study and practice. Sex is used for its mystical and magical properties and to alter the consciousness of the person being initiated.

However, such rites are performed only in private between two consenting adults, never in front of other Wiccans or anyone else. Coven orgies are nonexistent. Wicca is not a swing club; Sabbats and Esbats aren't excuses to have sex.

Those Wiccans who utilize sex in ritual—and they are by far in the minority—offer no apologies for doing so. They see Wicca as a fertility religion and so deem sex a natural component of its rituals. Centuries of Christian sexual repression, they say, are responsible for the public's horror of ritual sex as well as of sex itself in any of its forms.

Our morals are thrust upon us by the society in which we live. Our society is dominated by the idea that sex should be engaged in only by married couples and solely for procreative purposes. Therefore, sex for any other reason is deemed sinful, even by married couples. Combining it with religion, in the public's mind, is an "abomination."

But there are sexual elements in nearly every religion, even in Christianity. Most of the sexual aspects of Christianity have been forgotten, covered up with confusing translations or conveniently left out of the "authorized" version of the Bible. But they are there.

So a few Wiccans utilize sex as a joyous, energy-raising experience during ritual. But they do so alone with their partner. Wicca is not a sex religion, and many Wiccans don't integrate actual sex into their rituals.

What is sex, really? It is a union with the self, with another individual, with the human race as a whole, and with the deity or deities that created us. When viewed with an open mind, uncluttered by artificial morality, sexual rituals are indeed religious and sacred in the old pre-Christian sense of these words.

Wiccans don't believe that the pleasures and wonders of sex are unnatural or evil. The God and Goddess didn't create sexuality as a test of the goodness of humans. They see it as a joyous part of life, and so some Wiccans celebrate this in ritual.

Wicca is a unique religion, one with great variety. The fact that sex plays a role in *some* Wiccan covens and traditions doesn't mean that *all* Wiccans give it the same—or any—ritual importance.

Those who do see it as an act of love, power and spirituality.

## WICCAN MAGIC

So Wiccans worship the Goddess and God, have tools particular to their religion, perform seasonal and Lunar rites—and practice magic. Wiccans, in common with folk magicians, have been trained to manipulate personal energy. Wiccan magic follows the same rationale of folk magic, but the techniques may be far different.

Folk magicians may burn candles, manipulate quartz crystals or use herbs and oils to effect magical changes. Wiccan covens usually perform group-oriented rites involving the raising of energy.

The magic outlined here refers primarily to covens and groups of Wiccans. Solitary Wiccans may utilize similar rituals or practice folk magic while calling upon the Goddess and God to assist them.

The goals of Wiccan magic are often similar to those in folk magic. Healing is perhaps the most common objective along with love, finances, employment and protection. Curses and hexes are unknown. Wiccan magic also tackles larger problems, such as world peace.

Wiccan covens began working toward this goal in the late 1960s when it was common for covens to literally join forces in sending energy to halt the Vietnam War.

Another aim of Wiccan magic is to arrest exploitation of the Earth, to conserve natural resources and to send energy back to our planet in order to ensure its continued existence.

Wiccan methods of raising energy were long kept secret, revealed solely to coven members after initiation. Today, many of these have been openly published. Some are peculiar to Wicca.

## THE DANCE

The commonest form utilizes physical activity. The high priestess, high priest or some other coven leader discusses the goal of the magical rite to be performed with the group. When this is clearly in mind, they begin.

Within the magic circle the Wiccans join hands and move clockwise around the altar, visualizing or concentrating on the magical need. This has been called *the Dance* and it is the most common form of energy raising.

The coven circles faster and faster around the altar until it becomes a blur to the eyes. During this the Wiccans are steadily increasing their energy. At the appropriate time—when the coven's power has been raised to its peak—the group leader signals the members to release their energy and, through visualization, to direct it toward the goal. In some groups the members send their energy to the leader who directs the power outward.

If a folk magician can raise a sufficient amount of energy to effect magical changes, it follows that a group of persons, all working toward the same goal, can produce a tremendous amount of power. Group magical workings—whether Wiccan or not—can be spectacularly effective.

## CHANT THE SPELL

Other forms of Wiccan magic are similar. The coven usually is arranged in a circle. Members may stand still, link arms and chant or hum while visualizing the magical goal and raising personal energy. The leader, as before, determines when the available power is at its greatest concentration and again informs the coven to release its energy.

Other Wiccan groups may utilize variations on the above forms—or may even practice ceremonial magic to achieve their goals.

No matter what type of coven magic is used, it is usually effective.

## AN IT HARM NONE

Folk magic, as we have seen it, is governed by one basic dictum: Harm none. As a religion embracing magic, Wicca follows the same rule though it is often worded differently:

*"An it harm none, do what you will."*

(The *an* used here is an archaic form of if, not a variant of *and*.)

This phrase is known almost universally to English-speaking Wiccans. Its origins still remain shadowy. Many Wiccans feel that it was first phrased into these words during the 1940s or 50s and was based on the magical motto of ceremonial magician Aleister Crowley: "Do what thou wilt shall be the whole of the law. Love is the law; love under will."

While the origins of this phrase are misty, its message is not. As with folk magicians, Wiccans do not practice negative magic. They do not break up marriages, force persons to fall in love or harm others through their rituals. Sure, Wiccans get angry. They may get into fist fights or toss a drink in an obnoxious guy's face. But they'd rather cut off their right arm before "hexing" or "cursing" another person.

In the popular mind, magical power seems to be equated with the lack of morality. This is as absurd as thinking that the possession of a knife inclines its owner to stab everyone he or she meets. At best, true mastery of magical power only occurs in individuals who subscribe to the dictum "An it harm none, do what you will."

The possibility of the misuse of Wiccan magical techniques was one of the rationales for secrecy in the past: "Don't reveal magical methods to the untrained; they'll burn themselves and others." While there may have once been some logic behind this idea, it is no longer valid. Wiccan magical techniques have been openly published. Anyone with $10 (or a library card) can read most of these "secrets."

True, there probably have been some groups who called themselves Wiccan and who practiced negative magic. But to term these groups "Wiccans" would be as incorrect as calling those unfortunate souls who perform satirical masses and desecrate the host "true Catholics"—or Wiccans.

Wiccan magic is performed for positive ends and for coven members, for the coven as a whole, and for the Earth and all its peoples. It is a positive, participatory aspect of the religion of Wicca.

## DON'T CONVERT THE MASSES!

One of the areas in which Wicca greatly differs from most other contemporary, orthodox religions is in evangelism.

No Wiccan is pressured to be Wiccan. There is no threat of "eternal hellfire and damnation," no abyss after life, no retribution for not practicing Wicca. The Goddess and God aren't jealous deities, and Wiccans aren't frightened or subdued by them. Candidates for initiation do not renounce their former faith.

There is no sin, certainly not original sin, in Wicca. There is no heaven or hell. There are few rules save for that which also governs folk magic: Harm none.

What this means is that Wicca is a non-proselytizing religion. There are no Wiccan missionaries, no "witnesses," no Wiccans out recruiting others.

This may be surprising to those raised in orthodox religions, but it is based on a sound, true concept which is the antithesis of most other religions: *No one religion is right for everybody.*

Perhaps it's not too strong to say that the highest form of human vanity is the assumption that your religion is the only way to the Deity, that everyone will find it as fulfilling as you do, and that those with different beliefs are deluded, misled or ignorant.

It is understandable why many religions and their followers feel this way and participate in "converting the masses." Watching others change to their faith re-establishes that faith's correctness in the mind of the convertor. "If others believe, then I must not be deluding myself." Some members of orthodox religions truly are concerned for the soul of non-believers. But this is based on their religion's false teachings.

Another aspect of evangelism involves politics. If Religion *A* converts Country *B*, it increases its political and financial power in that country. The same is true of important persons. Orthodox religions have far-reaching influence in the realms of government and finance. Political candidates backed by major religions often are elected and propose or support legislation that furthers that religion's interest.

Money is a third reason for evangelism. Organized religions today in the United States take in billions of tax-free dollars every month. True, some of this money is spent on charitable causes, but the bulk of it pours into the faith's bureaucracy, benefitting the people who run it. So as more followers join, more money appears.

## THE FEWER, THE MERRIER

Wicca simply isn't like this. It is not organized to this extent. National groups do exist, but these are mainly for social and sometimes legal reasons. Gatherings of Wiccans may draw hundreds of people, but local covens usually number less than 10 members, and many Wiccans practice their religion entirely alone, with no group affiliations.

Wicca is not a financial institution and doesn't strive to become one. Students don't pay for initiations. Small fees, when they exist, are similar to dues required in any group to pay for supplies, refreshments, etc.

And so the stories of Witches (read Wiccans) belonging to a worldwide organization that aims to rule the world are false. So are the lies that Wiccans try to coerce others to join their religion. They simply aren't that insecure about their religion.

Don't worry; Wiccans aren't out roaming the streets plotting to force little Billy or your Aunt Sarah to join a coven.

Wicca is a religion for people who decide they belong in it.

## TROUBLE

Much like religions that exist in undeveloped countries, Wicca consists of small groups. They may meet in the countryside, on the beach, or in the mountains, but usually gather indoors. The reason? Public ignorance.

An example of this occurred quite recently. A Wiccan group in California decided to perform one of their rituals in a public park. Well in advance of the ritual, they had obtained the required meeting permit to avoid any unpleasant situations. The day arrived and the coven, wearing robes, set up their altar and began their simple rite.

Halfway through the ritual, somebody saw them and called the police. "Satanists," the informer said in an agitated voice. "Human sacrifice. Devil worship!

They're—they're killing babies in the park!" Several law enforcement officers soon arrived and rudely broke up the ritual. As the astonished Wiccans looked on helplessly, the officers disturbed the objects on the altar and began interrogating the coven members.

By the time the rightfully outraged Wiccans showed the officers their permit and convinced them they weren't about to commit murder, the ritual area was a shambles. All thoughts of proceeding with the ritual, or even of beginning again, were quickly forgotten.

Another variation on this theme occurred in the Midwest. A Wiccan group began hosting Esbats on their land in the countryside. Soon after news of their religious meetings spread, a staunch churchgoer decided that these members were Satanists. People interviewed by local newspapers informed reporters that they kept their children indoors on the nights of the Full Moon so that they wouldn't be killed by the Witches. Libelous allegations spread throughout the rural community for several weeks, all directed against a nature-loving, life-affirming religious group.

So persecution continues out of ignorance and lies.

## THE PROBLEMS OF SECRECY

As we've seen, Wicca was once a secret religion. Its rituals were performed far from prying eyes, certainly not in public parks. Interested persons were trained, sworn to secrecy and initiated into groups.

Some of the reasons for this secrecy are obvious, taking into account the above stories. Ignorant people can wreak havoc for contemporary Wiccans. Four hundred years ago members of these groups would have been legally executed, sending a glow of satisfaction through the populace. Even today, public disclosures of Wiccan membership can result in tragedy.

At least one Wiccan ended his life after his religion became publicly known. This wasn't from shame but from the emotional, psychological and financial persecution that resulted from this undesired, vicious revelation.

Being a Wiccan in this world isn't easy. Wiccans have been punched in the mouth on city streets for wearing pentagrams. They have been assaulted by rock-throwing, radical Christians. Wiccans have been burned out of their homes. They have lost jobs, housing, husbands and wives. Hate mail regularly arrives at their doors. Their children have been abducted by mates who misunderstood their religion.

Fundamentalist Christians picket outside Wiccan gatherings. Bomb threats are not unknown. Occasionally, Wiccans are even murdered for their religious beliefs. And over and over again they are accused of murder, Satan worship, cattle mutilation, orgies, and listening to rock-and-roll music!

Is it any wonder that many Wiccans continue to practice their religion in secrecy?

## THE SOLUTION

Many outsiders say that Wiccan secrecy covers up what they are *really* doing. Again, old misconceptions die hard. In light of the real dangers awaiting publicly known Wiccans, there seems to be only one solution to this problem: education. Tell the non-Wiccans what Wicca is about, many of them are saying. Assure them that Wiccans are normal, everyday citizens who just happen to practice a different religion. Let them know the truth about Wicca.

And so many Wiccans are emerging from the shadows. They write books about their religion, appear on television and speak to the public about Wicca. Frankly, some of them enjoy the attention they get. After all, they're only human.

Many of them have been persecuted for their trouble. All have been rewarded by a slow but growing understanding of Wicca among the masses. Perhaps Wicca hasn't been *accepted* in the United States as a viable, alternative religion. Neither has Shinto or Buddhism or many other unfamiliar religions. But the groundwork has been laid which is already providing positive results. The very fact that this book could be published and distributed is proof of that.

The Wiccans are speaking. The truth will out!

## AND THEN?

If, after reading this booklet, you wish to learn more about Wicca, the best way to start is by reading. Read every book you can find on the subject—both the good works and the bad. Read with a critical eye, evaluating each author individually. Be especially careful when reading works that contain numerous Biblical quotations. They're filled with outright lies and inaccuracies.

One of the newest Wiccan books is *Buckland's Complete Book of Witchcraft*. While fairly comprehensive, this book doesn't describe the practices and beliefs of every Wiccan. No one book could. But it does contain a wealth of information.

Remember that few Wiccans agree on ritual design, nudity, tools and coven organization. The same is true of Wiccan authors. Many Wiccan traditions are in diametric opposition to the methods of others. One of the currently "hot" topics is the ancient history—or lack thereof—of Wicca. So not all authors will describe Wicca in the same way. Even though they're all members of the same religion, each is an individual and belongs to various Wiccan traditions. It is a personal religion.

However, to be sure that the Wicca you are reading about is real, keep the information contained within this booklet in mind. If the authors speak of Satan worship, sacrifices, forced initiations and orgies, as well as many other unpleasant things, they are not Wiccans and the book is the product of a twisted mind. Consider the book a work of fiction.

If, after reading about Wicca you wish to learn more, try to find a Wiccan in your area. Few Wiccans advertise or publicly reveal their addresses, so it can be difficult to meet one. If you are serious about gaining entrance to Wicca, seek out every lead you can find.

Write to the authors of Wiccan books. Though you may not get a reply, information can occasionally be passed on that may help you. It's certainly worth the time and effort.

And remember—if you do contact someone through rather strange means and are told that you will soon become a true Satanist, that you have to renounce your former religion, that you have to pay for initiation, or that you must take drugs to participate in ceremonies, you are not in contact with a genuine Wiccan coven or person.

If you meet a Wiccan individual or coven that practices ritual nudity and/or ritual sex, and if this bothers you, simply reject them and look for another. The same is true if you feel a severe personality clash with any of the Wiccans you meet. Chances are they won't accept you anyway.

If you fail in your attempts to meet Wiccans, you may wish to begin practicing your religion alone. One book geared specifically to help solitary students is Scott Cunningham's *Wicca: A Guide for the Solitary Practitioner*. This is a complete introduction to the practice of Wicca, and is a reliable source for those unable to join a coven or otherwise receive training. Remember, such books are not proselytization. They are simply presenting authentic Wiccan information to those who are interested in receiving it. Keep looking. As the Wiccans often say, those who are ready for Wicca will find it.

## WHAT IT IS AND WHAT IT'S NOT

To sum up, Witchcraft today is folk magic: a gentle, ancient, constructive use of little-understood forces to effect positive changes.

This term also includes Wicca, a modern religion rooted in reverence of the Goddess and God and that respects nature. Magic is an accepted part of this religion, which has a number of traditions.

Folk magic is not cursing, hexing, blasting or other negative magic. It is not performed with powers derived from pacts with the Devil or Satan.

Wicca is not a parody, reversal or perversion of Christianity. It is also not an evangelical, controlling or proselytizing religion or cult. Wicca is not out to rule the world, convert your children, take your money or try to force you to believe as its followers do. Wicca is not anti-Christian; it is simply non-Christian.

Neither folk magicians nor Wiccans kill living beings. Nor are orgies a part of their religious and magical practices. These ideas are spread by persons who simply don't know the facts or who choose to ignore them for their own ends. Wiccans and folk magicians don't wish to be feared or converted; they just want to be left alone.

May everyone know the truth about Witchcraft.

Llewellyn publishes hundreds of books
on your favorite subjects.

# LOOK FOR THE CRESCENT MOON
to find the one you've been searching for!

To find the book you've been searching for, just call or write for a FREE copy of our full-color catalog, *New Worlds of Mind & Spirit*. *New Worlds* is brimming with books and other resources to help you develop your magical and spiritual potential to the fullest! Explore over 80 exciting pages that include:

- **Exclusive interviews, articles and "how-tos" by Llewellyn's expert authors**

- **Features on classic Llewellyn books**

- **Tasty previews of Llewellyn's latest books on astrology, Tarot, Wicca, shamanism, magick, the paranormal, spirituality, mythology, alternative health and healing, and more**

- **Monthly horoscopes by Gloria Star**

- **Plus special offers available only to *New Worlds* readers**

## To get your free *New Worlds* catalog, call 1-877-NEW-WRLD

or send your name and address to

**Llewellyn
P.O. Box 64383
St. Paul, MN
55164-0383**

Visit our web site at
www.llewellyn.com.

LLEWELLYN
*New Worlds of Mind and Spirit*